five seven five: a
daily glimpse of Chicago
life seen through haiku

David J.P. Fisher

Copyright ©2018 David J.P. Fisher
All Rights Reserved

Cover Design by Debbie O'Byrne at JETLAUNCH.net

Interior Design by JETLAUNCH.net and David J.P. Fisher

ISBN Paperback: 978-1-944730-07-9
ISBN E-Book: 978-1-944730-08-6

All rights reserved. Published in the United States by RockStar Publishing, Evanston, Illinois. No part of this book may be reproduced, scanned, or distributed in any printed or electronic form without written permission from the publisher. Please do not participate in or encourage piracy of copyrighted material in violation of the author's rights.

A RockStar Publishing Book

For my father,

who had a beret and a notebook full
of poetry before I ever showed up

Still summer sunshine
Bird rests, cat rests, my wife rests
I try writing poems

COME ALONG WITH ME

Haiku is a traditional form of poetry born in Japan. After five centuries, it's gone through a lot of evolutions and revolutions. It's a form that's been used by a lot of different poets in a lot of different ways. It can harness the… blah, blah, blah.

You can read the intro below if you'd like. Or. You can just skip to a random page, read the poem, and find out what it makes you see, feel, and think. I mean, c'mon, it's just poetry.

· · · ·

Ok, so you're hanging around. I had to add the disclaimer above because the first few drafts of this introduction were getting way too heady. It felt like I was writing a Wikipedia page for the book.

The Japanese poetry form that we recognize as haiku has been around for a long time, like over five hundred years. If you want to dig into the ways to interpret and understand haiku, there are fantastic books at the library (or you can Google it). But to give you a starting point if you are a haiku newbie, here's how I thought about the structure that informed how I approached my writing:

A good haiku works like a well-written joke by a stand-up comedian. There's a setup, where you create the framework and expectation. Then there's the punchline, where you deliver the often-unexpected payoff.

While haiku isn't usually written to be comedic, it is meant to illustrate a truth through observation. The original Japanese form relies on what is called a kireji, or cutting word, to juxtapose the first and second half of the poem. Since the structure of writing is different in English-language haiku, the break between the 2nd and 3rd lines often serve the same function. I also found myself using punctuation, spacing, or the reader's mental framework to create that juxtaposition.

But with 365 poems in this book, you can bet I sometimes took license with the form. Heck. That was half the fun.

· · · ·

There's a tradition of using haiku to sketch a journey. Some of the great writers of the form (like the master Basho - you should look him up if you enjoy haiku) used their poems to document their observations on the road while traveling throughout Japan.

This book came from much humbler origins, but it ended in a similar place. It started as a month-long challenge that I had given myself to write a haiku every day. It was an attempt to get back to the creative writing that I enjoyed but had gotten away from. These days, my writing time is much more focused on books and online articles about business and sales. Interesting topics, but ones that don't really lend themselves to soulful reflection.

At some point in that first month, I decided I would try to write one haiku a day for a year. As I stretched out the challenge over the months, I realized that I was also documenting a journey. It wasn't one through space, it was through time. As I "stood" in one place, the world changed around me.

Chicago was a perfect backdrop for this project. It was (and is) a complex landscape that seemed to hold everything. There's the natural beauty of the lake and parks, the soaring steel and concrete buildings, the hustle of millions of people who have been drawn in from around the world. There's just a lot going on.

Seeing how all these things fit together, sometimes smoothly and sometimes not so smoothly, created a powerful canvas to explore the nuances of life.

[By the way, I don't technically have a Chicago address. I live on the border; my alley splits Evanston and Chicago. But I do spend a few days a week working and playing there - as evidenced by all my public transportation poems. And for several years, I not only lived in Chicago, I lived 2 houses from an El track. I just want to head off any of the haters complaining I have the wrong zip code.]

· · · ·

While many of the feelings, thoughts, and experiences contained in these poems will hopefully resonate for you, this was still my very personal and idiosyncratic trip around the sun. We don't always remember the years that don't have a birth, death, or birthday that ends in a 0, but maybe that's why this was such a valuable project.

Many things happened over the year I was writing. All if it important, but none of it earth-shattering.

My wife and I experienced the ups and downs of trying to start a family, my mother was quite sick and spent a good amount of time in the hospital, and I worked to build my consulting business. The political climate of the country continued to be, um, tense. And I even tried to teach myself Spanish.

Those experiences are reflected in the poems – and you will probably be able to guess when they fell in the year. Even though they are personal, the emotions of sadness, excitement, disappointment, anger, and gratitude are probably ones that you can relate to as well.

On another level, I was also exploring concepts like impermanence, awareness, and meaning. Not because I wanted to be needlessly deep, but because they are topics that I am wrestling with in my life. I have a feeling you might be trying to figure out some of these areas as well.

· · · ·

I've included short excerpts from a journal I kept where I documented my thoughts at the beginning of each month. They'll give you an idea of where my mindset was and can clue you in to how I was approaching writing at that specific point in the process.

But don't let that cloud your perspective too much. You can find the meaning in it that you want. Haiku is very much about the current moment. The form focuses on mindfulness and paying attention to what the writer is observing in the here and now. Likewise, it's also about what the reader is experiencing in the moment.

There's no right or wrong way to read a haiku.

This is now your book, not mine.

· · · ·

That being said, I would challenge you to look beyond the initial image that's presented. It's just a starting point. After the initial reading, try to build the scene in your mind. It will obviously be different than the one I saw, but that's fine. It's your image.

Then ask yourself: How did this scene get here? What will happen in this moment? What might happen next? What is the feeling that comes when I hold this image in my mind?

Some of these pieces are meant to look at fundamental parts of the human experience. And some of them are simply a chance to observe the beauty, mundanity, or insubstantial nature of our surroundings. If you read a poem and it sticks in your mind, that's great. And if you think, "Ah, that's interesting", and that's it, well, then that's the perfect response. I've always tried to be clear with my writing. I think it makes little sense to bury a message underneath convoluted layers of imagery and intent.

Here's my hope for you: That after reading one of these haiku (or bingeing a whole month), you will be able to put the book down and look out at the moment you are inhabiting with slightly different eyes. And that in doing so, you find your own path through the world a little more interesting, instructive, or inspiring.

So let's go.

AUGUST 1

Cafe patio
My chair and table inside
Waits for my return

湿度

AUGUST 2

Dusk. Clear view. Slight breeze.
Torrential downpour. Start. Stop.
Sky remains unmoved

湿度

AUGUST 3

Dawn humidity
Not knowing to come or go
Whoosh! squirrel runs by

湿度

AUGUST 4

Coffehouse noises
Grinding, bad music, television
Wind laughing outside

湿度

AUGUST 5

What makes a leaf move?
The masters would say my mind.
But I'm passing through.

湿度

AUGUST 6

Dawn sun comes early
Lighting minds still wanting sleep
Grass grows where it will

湿度

AUGUST 7

Green garden leaves burst,
among late summer ripeness.
Listen. Your seeds echo

湿度

AUGUST 8

Full moon hangs alone
illuminates my bedroom
dark is relative

湿度

AUGUST 9

grave markers at dusk
bright faces and long shadows
my ice cream melts fast

湿度

AUGUST 10

empty pepper plant
too much wind? too little sun?
it chuckles at me

湿度

AUGUST 11

Street side happy hour
Honking, music, wind, noise, beer
Rain clouds come and go

湿度

AUGUST 12

Suburb meat contest
Best rack in the culdesac
Winning is losing

湿度

AUGUST 13

Blue sky, white clouds, and
green grass. Try making them more
than they want to be.

湿度

AUGUST 14

Jewels dance on waves
Flashing transcendence
Coarse sand in my toes

湿度

AUGUST 15

Winter will still come
Spring is before and after
Now, humidity

湿度

AUGUST 16

Cicadas chirrrup
Background noise exists unseen
Cat licks her paws clean

湿度

AUGUST 17

dusk hides behind clouds
gray with promises of rain
neither sun nor moon

湿度

AUGUST 18

Tires cut through wet streets.
The sound cuts through my zazen.
So where is the rain?

湿度

AUGUST 19

Summer festival
Music carried on warm breeze
Is this not nature?

湿度

AUGUST 20

Sunday morning pause
After Saturday night play
The Irish know Zen

湿度

AUGUST 21

Solar eclipse that
the people scrambled to view.
Sun didn't notice.

湿度

AUGUST 22

lightning bursts and strikes
white night fades to black night. don't
chase enlightenment

湿度

AUGUST 25

Green leaf or no leaf
Golden leaf or budding leaf.
World rushes through space

湿度

AUGUST 26

Cat in a window
Watching birds and cars pass by
Mountains rarely move

湿度

AUGUST 27

Geese stroll in the park
Eat, shit, repeat. Only we
walk on their droppings

湿度

AUGUST 28

Sunlight breaks through glass,
hits eyes trapped by warm blankets.
Does Monday exist?

湿度

AUGUST 29

Invisible wind.
Bending trees. Blowing dark clouds.
Not all storms are seen.

湿度

AUGUST 30

Afternoon. August.
Abstractions built by my mind.
Sun creates heat now.

湿度

AUGUST 31

Droning cicadas
Background unseen until gone
Just like my zazen

湿度

SEPTEMBER

"Why are you writing haiku?"

That's been the common question this month. I started out wanting to add a creative task to my monthly list of goals. I'm trying to flex my fiction writing muscles after writing so much non-fiction, and I'm still drawn to the idea of going back to the Poetry Slam at the Green Mill. Unfortunately, I still also want to keep up with my non-fiction writing (which pays the bills), and all of those things take time.

What doesn't take as much time?

Seventeen syllables.

When I've posted the haiku on Facebook, the responses have been quite varied. Some people find them funny, some cute, and some morbid. It makes me realize that most people don't really take the time to think deeply about the world that surrounds them. My first goal is to use this project to create that introspection opportunity for myself. The second is to give another person, whoever they are, the glimpse that might help them on their path.

We'll see if I can write for another month. In the end, it's just seventeen symbols a day.

SEPTEMBER 1

Slight nip in the air
Unseasonably chilly
The gravestones don't mind

SEPTEMBER 2

Here at summer's end
Yellow wildflowers burst forth.
Joy has no season.

SEPTEMBER 3

Form is emptiness
doesn't mean you won't enjoy
summer by the lake.

SEPTEMBER 4

Last day of 40.
39 years spent fearing.
Now sadly, goodbyes.

SEPTEMBER 5

Each is a birth day
Every day I'm new. But
Only one has cake.

SEPTEMBER 6

Cold floor on bare feet
Sniff of cool air under warm
Every flame must die

SEPTEMBER 7

Cold air can chill bones.
Unseen wind can blow branches.
What ghosts haunt your mind?

SEPTEMBER 8

Ducks scattered on pond
Afloat on choppy water
Lake beyond is grey

SEPTEMBER 9

Dawning sun glares gold
Bouncing bright on crashing waves
Our truth waits daily

SEPTEMBER 10

No storm here. Elsewhere,
Winds and rains tear through the skies.
One world. Not many.

SEPTEMBER 11

stolen summer night
strung lights twinkle above us
one last outdoor beer

SEPTEMBER 12

From my morning view,
Today's temp could go anywhere.
A sweater or no?

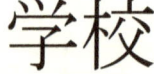

SEPTEMBER 13

Post noon café crowd
Different faces, same thirst
Caffeine knows no clock

SEPTEMBER 14

citywide El map
rainbow veins draw to Loop heart
I am here. Am I?

学校

SEPTEMBER 15

Dawn light hangs sideways
Throwing shadows on the wall
Wait! Don't look east now.

SEPTEMBER 16

Sailboats skim the lake
Blown by wind, it blows my hair.
Countless sands, one beach

学校

SEPTEMBER 17

Lake is calm today.
Clouds filter soft morning sun
Joggers don't notice

SEPTEMBER 18

Wake from dream to dream.
Daytime feeling of control
the sole difference

SEPTEMBER 19

Constitutional
Each morning, what comes in, out
Inevitable

SEPTEMBER 20

lawnmower out there,
traffic on street, sounds surround.
mind is louder still

SEPTEMBER 21

Zazen on the moon?
Beyond Dogen's horizon.
A wall is a wall.

SEPTEMBER 22

Equinox heat wave
Less than summer, more than fall
Geese still flee southward

SEPTEMBER 23

Gold, orange, yellow, pink
Sunlight has many colors
I enjoy them all

SEPTEMBER 24

Morning should bring food
Can opener still in bed
Meow meow meow meow meow

SEPTEMBER 25

Pine tree next to oak.
One has temporary leaves.
Spring will come for both.

SEPTEMBER 26

What is more fickle?
Nature's moods in Chicago,
Or our preference

学校

SEPTEMBER 27

Cold front moves over,
Grey and cool. Sun sets early.
My mood is my choice.

SEPTEMBER 28

Bears Packers contest
Midwest rite, troubled future
Some gods should be sacked

SEPTEMBER 29

El rumbles above
Concrete pillars rot below
Blind men fall off cliffs

SEPTEMBER 30

Birds, bunnies, squirrels!
Backyard circus in high gear.
What part can I play?

OCTOBER

…The writing itself has continued to evolve and challenge. I'm definitely past the honeymoon phase and there have been a few days where I don't really want to have to write anything or I have no idea where inspiration will come from. Conversely, there are days where I can't focus during my morning meditation because my mind keeps riffing opening lines.

I've been letting go of my need to be "deep" or esoteric in the lines. If it happens, great. But I also have to realize that any past master was still just writing about what he or she saw in their moments. So if I write about a football game or my morning bathroom trip, that's just as valid as a poem about a mist-covered landscape.

I'm also enjoying the interplay of nature with the "natural" world of the city. Sure, the train tracks are man-made, but that's as much a part of my environment as the tree growing outside my living room window.

As the months go by, I'm sure I'll repeat subjects and ideas, and that's OK. I'll probably also get to the point that I used to while doing improv comedy, where my pre-conceived notions are used up. That will be a good place to get to because then I'll be able to create some spontaneous work. But in the meantime, I'm trying to just run with ideas that pop up…

OCTOBER 1

Afternoon shadows
Cast by trees, people, steeples
Lengthening, then gone

OCTOBER 2

photo worthy sky
magazine cover sunset
small win for dark day

OCTOBER 3

Gentle breeze, strong gust
Unseen agents ruffle leaves
What pushes me here?

OCTOBER 4

stone just sits still
awash in rain and sunlight
still just sitting

OCTOBER 5

Neighbor voices shout
passion, anger, frustration
Thin walls between us

OCTOBER 6

Lone oak sentinel
Brown cornstalks wait the combine
It will stand next spring

OCTOBER 7

Empty childhood home
waits for new childhoods to house.
I'll keep the stairs' creak.

OCTOBER 8

Warm lap. Purring cat.
She found the spot she wanted.
We each play a part

OCTOBER 9

each night, Miss Spider
spins her web and lives in it
my mind spins stories

OCTOBER 10

sharp winds drive grey clouds
promising rain. suggesting
pedal fast, stay dry

OCTOBER 11

solid flat gray sky
blank canvas as much as blue
must draw my own sun

OCTOBER 12

night clouds glowing pink
reflect light from city streets
do stars wait above

OCTOBER 13

Basho's eludes me
His craft years and miles distant
Cardinal sings sweet

OCTOBER 14

3:00 am lightning,
Photo negative of night.
Flash! The real waits.

葉

OCTOBER 15

Wind buffets branches
Tosses leaves back and forth
Trunk stands in stillness

OCTOBER 16

Garden between rails
Gravel, weeds, flowers, refuse
Tended by chance winds

OCTOBER 17

Squirrel hides his nut
and then forgets it. Maybe.
Chance births tallest oaks

OCTOBER 18

Cat's fuzzy belly
Slow up and down in sunbeam.
Practicing wu wei

OCTOBER 19

Flying birds look up.
Expect empty sky, not us.
Do we amuse them?

OCTOBER 20

Land of perfect squares
Drawn before dreams of flying
We can be clever

OCTOBER 21

Unseen can be strong
Wind knocks over my beer glass
Ships tack or sail back

OCTOBER 22

fall Chicago rain
like Galway's: gray, cold, windblown
countered with warm pubs

OCTOBER 23

Don't believe old books
There are no death astronauts
Squirrels know more truth

OCTOBER 24

Deep blue pre-dawn sky
Not black night or high noon bright
Balanced in a point

OCTOBER 25

Rows of parked El trains
Glint bright in a gravel lot.
Waiting for meaning

OCTOBER 26

Inebriated.
I'm buzzed on beer, while you are
Drunk on your own thoughts

OCTOBER 27

Jammed bike chain taunts me
Stuck in gears and wheel for now
Choose walking. That works.

OCTOBER 28

Death mystifies us
Carved pumpkins and fake cobwebs
We are living fools

OCTOBER 29

Sun slipping under
Tomorrow comes from behind
New now comes around

OCTOBER 30

Shortening days
Bring complaints and bemoaning
Are your minutes filled?

OCTOBER 31

Post-zombie attack
I scavenge suburb garage.
Chock full of nothing.

NOVEMBER

…The oomph of a new project has worn off. Now it's just a slog to keep going. Some days the poems come easy, sometimes I don't want to write anything. So this is where the discipline starts kicking in. I find it helpful to have a reminder pop up on my phone every day to remind me. But most days I don't need it.

What I have found is that even on the days that I don't know what to write, if I just slow down for just a moment, and look around, something pops up. And idea takes form in my mind because I notice a tree, a bird, or even just a thought that has been sitting there, waiting.

I'm also letting go of the idea that I have to write my poems with the esoteric feel of a Basho haiku. I still try it sometimes, but I'm trying to play around with the form a little. I'm branching out from using only capitalization and punctuation for line breaks, and I'm having more fun with the language itself…

風

NOVEMBER 1

Bare feet on cold floor
Dawn walk to sitting pillow
Cold feet on bare floor

NOVEMBER 2

Grey sky, clouds inside.
Unstoppable inner sun
returns tomorrow

NOVEMBER 3

same tree, every day
seen out my window, but not
every day, new eyes

NOVEMBER 4

Saturday chore list
plans to hold back entropy
each and every week

NOVEMBER 5

Daylight savings time.
How do I save some sunshine
For future dark days?

NOVEMBER 6

Make every moment
Monday, the past falls away
Now begin again

NOVEMBER 7

We see rampant waves
of fall color and beauty
Trees just do their thing

NOVEMBER 8

Sun wars against clock
Over who controls the time
Dark night comes early

NOVEMBER 9

snow leopard paces
caged beauty and lithe power
with regular meals

NOVEMBER 10

Light dusting of snow
Grey haze of flakes, wind, and clouds
Spring lies at it's heart

NOVEMBER 11

Awake early morn
Poised to get the worm quicker
Baristas laugh first

NOVEMBER 12

Sunday stretches on
Between last week and the next
Finite endlessness

NOVEMBER 13

afternoon playground
emptied by chill and classrooms
wind pushes one swing

NOVEMBER 14

squirrels bury nuts
future meals, or future trees
each hole filled with hope

NOVEMBER 15

Liminal grayness
Stuck between light/dark, wet/dry
Who will unstuck it?

NOVEMBER 16

Possibility
is a joy and a sadness
living together

NOVEMBER 17

Lit planes float in line
Above dark Lake Michigan
While I walk homeward

NOVEMBER 18

Time
is a shared delusion that
ends all things.

NOVEMBER 19

Freshly painted walls
feel good. Enjoy them before
they start getting scuffed.

NOVEMBER 20

brick fits into brick
becoming sidewalks and walls
day fits into day

NOVEMBER 21

Pints raised in goodbyes
to Nevin's last last call. Fond
memories linger.

NOVEMBER 22

Train conductor tries
Moving holiday weekend
travelers homeward.

NOVEMBER 23

One thanksgiving day
Or countless mindful moments?
Turkey wants a say.

NOVEMBER 24

wind whips water rough
on the north side of the bay
south side remains calm

NOVEMBER 25

Timeless Saturday
afternoon fight: get chores done
or nap on the couch?

NOVEMBER 26

Cat lays next to me
while I sit. She starts purring
and I glimpse the Way

NOVEMBER 27

I marveled at the
trees' colors just weeks ago
and now they are bare.

NOVEMBER 28

If these days are gray,
at least they are short. But the
sunny days will be too.

NOVEMBER 29

Fall sniffles hit me.
I wish I could write haiku
Like my nose makes snot.

NOVEMBER 30

presidents and kings
have always been fools - so are
we if we're surprised

DECEMBER

…I see this exercise as a documentation of my journey. The only difference is that it's one through time instead of space. Just like the movie trick where a person stands still at center stage and events happen around them in fast motion, I feel that I'm here in the center and that events happen around me.

So these poems are a travelogue of my journey through my days as seen with a time-lapse camera. The time it takes to get from one day to the next in my life is 24 hours, in this book, it's only the flip of the page.

I'm also struck by the importance of keeping the poems grounded. Basho wasn't writing about rarified air. One of his poems about seeing "washer women" stands out. It reminds me of Ikkyu writing about the bar and the brothel. It's about paying attention to the mundane and finding the meaning in them. It's why I think the poems about snot and morning constitutionals are some of the "deepest" I've written, once you get past the initial awkwardness.

On a related note, I'm glad that the season has really started to change. I'm waiting for some snow. Fresh ideas!

DECEMBER 1

two young girls chatter
about problems real to them
geese fly south overhead

DECEMBER 2

full moon hung fat just
across trees from setting sun
two spheres competed

DECEMBER 3

Pale frost lays on grass,
reflects dawn light off headstones.
the dead don't notice

DECEMBER 4

The universe can't
see because it has no eyes.
It can borrow mine.

DECEMBER 5

Lone leaf clings to branch
Wind shakes lamppost back and forth
Earth hurtles through space

DECEMBER 6

summer skirts and shorts
are put away - train full of
walking winter coats

DECEMBER 7

wet leaves fill the curb
ears tingle with the cold air
bus thunders by me

DECEMBER 8

bright sun on cold day
mixed signals through my senses
leashed dog moves slowly

DECEMBER 9

Lakefront in layers
Blue gray, sage green, dirty white
Melancholy world

DECEMBER 10

cluttered expanse splits
Brewtown and Chitown - taillights
have replaced prairie

DECEMBER 11

poems without place
are
formless and empty

DECEMBER 12

Fat snowflakes hurry
past circles of streetlamp light
Snoopy plays Greensleeves

DECEMBER 13

Wednesday morning turned
to afternoon then night. My
mind blinked and missed it.

DECEMBER 14

Hibernating bears
Dream. When cold traps me at home
Work keeps me busy

DECEMBER 15

Cafe window stands
between bright warmth and grey world.
Both see the other.

DECEMBER 16

No matter the time
the sun sets - it is always
nature's spectacle

DECEMBER 17

Long winter evening
Lamp shines from a square window
What life is lived there?

DECEMBER 18

What makes a christmas
tree? the ornaments, the lights,
the gifts underneath?

夜

DECEMBER 19

Running for the train.
But that's my choice. More will come.
I don't want to wait.

DECEMBER 20

People shuffle past
this corner hunched in winter
coats going somewhere

DECEMBER 21

once it was a god
now Sun goes to sleep early
Moon hides within clouds

DECEMBER 22

People can't decide:
Hectic holiday errands?
Ignore work and chill?

DECEMBER 23

Deepest winter day
I let the sun warm my face
Small blackbird flies by

DECEMBER 24

Snow blurs distance. Flakes
cling to eyelashes. Falcon
swoops inches from ground.

夜

DECEMBER 25

Christmas memories
Strands of lights from then til now
Boardgames keep us warm

DECEMBER 26

Wind chills to below
zero - sun glints off whiteness
I will stay inside

DECEMBER 27

Cold creeps through my coat
Frozen breath hangs before me
Mailman walks his route

DECEMBER 28

Clean your closets.
Our journeys to far off lands
are bound to their start.

DECEMBER 29

Calendar changes
New numbers on a blank grid
Cat won't leave my lap

DECEMBER 30

pale wisps sweep from roofs
white against crisp blue, too much
wind to curl gently

DECEMBER 31

Time and space are joined.
Is a new year a new place?
If my mind allows.

JANUARY

…I've been thinking about how esoteric or straightforward I should be. When reading some of Basho's work, I was struck by how exotic some of his imagery is, and how down-to-earth it is in other areas. But I have to remind myself that a lot of what feels particularly strange is because it is about a different time and country. Cherry blossoms might strike me as an exotic image, but to one of his readers, it would just be a reminder of a certain time of year.

I remind myself that my personal style has always been to be straightforward in my writing. If I'm too obtuse, it doesn't do its job of communicating. At the same time, I also know that I shouldn't spoon-feed the reader. They should have to put some effort into deciphering it for themselves. I don't want them to have to guess at the meaning, I want them to understand my meaning. Then I want their next step to be the wrestling with that meaning: do they have a counter-image or does it affect them differently on an emotional level?

I've been thinking a lot about the hypothesis in physics that everything in the universe stands still, and instead, the observer moves through it over time. It's as if we have a small peep-hole and the universe passes by it.

I have a small peep-hole, and the whole universe passes by me.

JANUARY 1

Holidays are done
A new year is beginning
I sit on the couch

JANUARY 2

Bus bounces along
Salt stained cars jostle for space
Traffic light stops that

JANUARY 3

Woman drenched in fur
Shaggy yeti on the train
Boots covered in salt

JANUARY 4

Calm river surface
Blue amid white winter snow
Somehow unfrozen

JANUARY 5

Does zero degrees
mean temperature ceases
to exist? We're cold.

JANUARY 6

cafe patio
no chairs, only snow and cold
tea warms me inside

JANUARY 7

highway stretches north
connects homes to each other
sleet streaks the windshield

JANUARY 8

Temperature above
freezing for a moment. Now
thirty three feels warm.

JANUARY 9

waves lap away ice
damp haze moves in from the west
days change without help

JANUARY 10

spider walks slowly
across my window - warm winds
counterfeit springtime

JANUARY 11

after eleven sunsets
year has lost its new year smell
clear eyes see farther

JANUARY 12

Flurries shoot sideways,
Upwards, snowflakes blow about
Drifts crunch underfoot

JANUARY 13

potted herbs still green
resting on the windowsill
light comes in, not cold

JANUARY 14

Sunday, 4:30
Another long dark tea time
I'll retry post-nap

JANUARY 15

Grey winter rush hour
Snow and ice and impatience
Slower is faster

JANUARY 16

Sunset bounces off
snow covered rooftops. Takes me
back to Thai beaches

JANUARY 17

Lone grill, snow clad yard
Bare trees, empty bird feeder
Wind whips dormant grass

JANUARY 18

Phone alarm goes off
"Write a poem!" it tells me
Thoughts come on their own

JANUARY 19

water drips from awning
momentary melting snow
slow man missed the train

JANUARY 20

Sun hangs just past Dawn
Turning potential to real
What will this day bring?

JANUARY 21

Dark grey trees emerge
from clouds of fog. Streetlights glow
within wet halos.

JANUARY 22

My computer crashed
Warm winter weather is weird
Mondays can be off

JANUARY 23

Rain last night, snow now
White streaks slant before my eyes
Bedroom stays toasty

JANUARY 24

Metal boxes stretch
Upwards from squared street corners
People cross mid-block

JANUARY 25

Millions of souls
A drop in the universe
Sweet home Chicago

JANUARY 26

Mid winter palette
Greys, browns, greens, blues seen through a
dirt smudged train window

JANUARY 27

People filled lakefront
Stealing out of season warmth
Early moon joins us

JANUARY 28

lone lamp in alley
catch a glimpse of dog walkers
they go, the light stays

JANUARY 29

Night fades, black to blue
I sit here on my pillow
And try for the same

JANUARY 30

Thoughts come unbidden
at 6:00 am. They don't stick
around for sunrise.

JANUARY 31

One block away. The train!
...don't run. Late for this one is
early for the next

FEBRUARY

…I'm excited to look back at poems and see the path that they take through the year. It's hard to see the day-to-day effects of weather, holidays, and the like when you are living it. But the power of journaling is to capture the moment and let you revisit it. January has been a month of holiday hangover, bitter cold, greyness, and a bit of ennui. And I think that will come through. I haven't felt very, well, "light" this month, and that is coming through as well. But that's OK.

At first, I was nervous about repetition, but then I realized that life is full of it. It's not a totally new experience every day. Much of what we do, we've done before. The hope is that our experience of the sameness does change a bit over time, or at least evolves and matures. But in the end, the sun comes up every morning, I've missed the train more than once, and I try to sit in meditation daily.

Have I learned any lessons now that I'm at the halfway point? Even though the year is cyclic, I'm not sure if this is a journey that leads back to the beginning or to a whole new place. Either I'm as far away from my starting point as I'll be, or I'm truly just at a rest stop as I go further away from where I started.

I don't have any wisdom to impart to my future self from the half-way point. I guess the most important thing to remember on any journey: wherever you are, enjoy it. And then keep walking.

FEBRUARY 1

and sometimes Thursday
just rushes by in a blur
sunset comes quickly

FEBRUARY 2

Friday happy hour
So good when it hits your lips
Monday comes again

鼠色

FEBRUARY 3

winter storm comes soon
that's what the weatherman says
there's no snow today

鼠色

FEBRUARY 4

Snowy haze thrown up
Train rushing through white landscape
Mom turns seventy

鼠色

FEBRUARY 5

Walking in falling
snow changes the sound of life
one octave slower

鼠色

FEBRUARY 6

Points of light sparkle
On top of fresh snow - my mom
Passed seven decades

FEBRUARY 7

Homeless man huddles
on the El. Not mad enough
to huddle outside

鼠色

FEBRUARY 8

Train platform filled with
passengers. They wait to be
anywhere but right here

鼠色

FEBRUARY 9

I pile snow next to
the sidewalk with my shovel.
I could wait til spring.

鼠色

FEBRUARY 10

You can't move quickly,
When a snow day shuts things down.
Stop! Smell the roses.

FEBRUARY 11

Snow stacks on shoveled
walks. Now nature just teases us!
Squirrels sleep snuggly.

FEBRUARY 12

And after every
blizzard the sun comes out to
make the snow dazzle.

鼠色

FEBRUARY 13

in a winter night
each window shares a story –
pass without looking

FEBRUARY 14

Would your valentine
want a card or compassion?
What would you ask for?

鼠色

FEBRUARY 15

Forty two degrees.
Whether warm or cold depends
on what month it is.

FEBRUARY 16

Watching the morning
Starbucks line...always ten deep
Zombies pulled daily

FEBRUARY 17

falling flakes cover
gravestones across the alley
such winter beauty!

FEBRUARY 18

Flag sputters dully
Cowardly winds control it
Too many moms cry

鼠色

FEBRUARY 19

Broadway and Lawrence
blinking lights keep calling me
jazz floats through the door

FEBRUARY 20

my poems are sun,
lake, wind, train, rain, bird, tree, street -
what more is there?

鼠色

FEBRUARY 21

Concrete sidewalk squares
Pass under my shoes. Oak tree's
Branches split wildly

鼠色

FEBRUARY 22

imagination
my mind conjures a warm beach
I don't need sunblock

FEBRUARY 23

Friday night dinner
Line between week and weekend
A chance to exhale

FEBRUARY 24

Saturday morning -
Meant for relaxing or chores?
Instead, I write poems.

鼠色

FEBRUARY 25

the final cleaning -
passing on our childhood home
strong winds blow outside

鼠色

FEBRUARY 26

Monday morning sex
a wonderful antidote
for Monday morning

FEBRUARY 27

Freak warm front moves through
The birds enjoy the sun – I'm
a little worried

鼠色

FEBRUARY 28

salt stains my nice shoes
other months would have more days
but this one is done

MARCH

It's early in the morning on March 1st, and it's raining. But considering it might turn to snow later, that's not that bad – it was 60 degrees two days ago. It's a fitting way to exit February which was a month of extremes. Between a blizzard which dumped a foot of snow on Chicago in a day, the aforementioned warm front, and another school shooting that has taken over the political discussion of the country, there were a lot of things happening this month.

Often I come across a sight or an experience and that drives that poem. This month, there were days when I knew that I wanted to express a thought or give voice to an emotion. The challenge was then to be open to what was around me. That way I could find the representative element in the world to use as a vehicle. Honestly, it took extra time. But I was also rewarded with some poignant pieces

It reminded me of the versatility of haiku and poetry in general. It's not any more valid to write about intensely personal issues or societal issues - to be abstract or concrete, broad or incredibly specific.

That's what our life is. Our journey throughout our lives, years, and really days, is a bouncing between different perspectives and lenses. We read a newspaper or Facebook post about something that angers us about international politics, and then we have a conversation with a family member, and then we get hungry, and then we notice our mortality because of a receding hairline in the mirror. And that can all be in 20 minutes…

MARCH 1

wakened while rain drops
slide down my window - sun comes
from inside today

MARCH 2

Keys changed hands today.
The house is no longer ours.
We can make new homes.

MARCH 3

afternoon tacos
on Clark St. - we're the only
gringos in the place

MARCH 4

upstairs kids racing,
next door neighbors shout - I try
to sit in stillness

MARCH 5

Cold invades my hands
while I walk to the train - gloves
forgotten at home

MARCH 6

I have things to do.
The cat on my lap doesn't.
I'll listen to her.

MARCH 7

Fellow riders stare
at phones and miss the sunbeams
poking from the clouds.

MARCH 8

moon forgot to set
faded against the dawn sky
old thoughts linger still

MARCH 9

Sun paints clouds orange, pink
twilight sky blue, grey, green
Another week gone

MARCH 10

observatory
stars - light thousands of years old
- my needs appear short

MARCH 11

Spending daylight saved
since winter's height – Nobody
knows when bedtime is.

MARCH 12

Political signs
pepper lawns - In front of streets
littered with potholes

MARCH 13

March flurries make a
real world snow globe. Pretty. Trees
patiently waiting.

MARCH 14

sun stretching longer
students walk from their classrooms
spring isn't here...yet

MARCH 15

stretch of hard packed grass
patches of dull dormant green
unseen roots promise

MARCH 16

Green Mill happy hour
Blind man shows how to see jazz
And let the week go

MARCH 17

Cheers to those who came
and come to melt in the pot.
They get the job done.

MARCH 18

Swim laps on Sunday.
Water and week take effort.
End where I started.

MARCH 19

Chilled winds blast my face
Puts a lie to the bright sun
Last falls leaves whip by

MARCH 20

children swing on swings
outside my polling station -
ballots not bullets

MARCH 21

calendar says spring
one day past the equinox
feels like a Wednesday

MARCH 22

3:30 arrives
schoolkids clamor for snacktime
I stare into space

MARCH 23

birds chirp in the tree
outside my bedroom window
cat found the sunbeam

MARCH 24

How many times have
I stood at the El platform
looking down the track?

MARCH 25

green pine, naked oak
fat rabbit nibbles dead grass
children march for truth

MARCH 26

My cat talks to birds
fluttering by the window.
I type out emails.

MARCH 27

Rush hour El train full
of people, not eye contact.
I smile at strangers.

MARCH 28

Google tracks where I
write these lines. Do they see my
soul in their data?

MARCH 29

seder meal, easter
candy...cold, muddy, grey ground
whispers my rebirth

MARCH 30

Sun promises spring
My cold holds me in winter
formless clouds drift

MARCH 31

Brown leaves still linger
Branches wait this season's buds
Do they miss last year's

APRIL

…At this point I don't even need the reminder that pops up on my phone. I always have this itch at the back of my mind that needs to be scratched. "Have you written your haiku yet? Do you know what you want to write about? Stop. Look around. Do you see any inspiration?"

Even as I write these lines I'm pausing to look out my office window to see if anything strikes me. Which is a little ironic because I've now looked out that window hundreds of times (at last it feels that way). And yes, it has changed through the seasons, but it's also the same landscape that I'm mining for inspiration. After almost 250 haiku, it seems that there is little I haven't written about.

At the same time, I feel like I've only scratched the surface. I am playing around more with the starting point of an idea that

I want to share than with just the physical image that I want to share. It doesn't always happen that way, but since I've written so many poems I feel like I can do whatever I want now. I want to write about both larger and smaller topics because I think I've got the middle covered...

APRIL 1

loud family dinners
we wear roles like worn out clothes
who am I today?

誕生

APRIL 2

April Fool's Day is past.
It was yesterday. Buddha
statue smiles at me.

誕生

APRIL 3

Puddle sits idly.
Plop. Plop. Drops fall into it.
Ripples flash and die.

誕生

APRIL 4

snow greets my waking
a thin film on a spring morn
already melting

誕生

APRIL 5

Metra, Divvy, Lyft
CTA - connect stops
between home and home

APRIL 6

birds talk, train rumbles
elsewhere, traffic dully vrooms
city sights unseen

誕生

APRIL 7

potholes and orange cones -
decay and repair - Clark Street -
slalom down the road

誕生

APRIL 8

Afternoon couch nap
Pause between chores and workweek
Sunday mindfulness

誕生

APRIL 9

snow on lily shoots
white on green a rare beauty
winter coat weighs heavy

誕生

APRIL 10

five o'clock: walk by
joggers, dog-walkers, traffic,
lone unicyclist

誕生

APRIL 11

sky colored hazy
I try but can't name it's hue.
riding the red line

APRIL 12

Lie in bed pre dawn
Junkman rolls through the alley
I have thoughts for him

誕生

APRIL 13

Pigeons fill the trees
next to Picasso's sculpture.
They prefer branches.

APRIL 14

waves crash the lakefront
winds drive rain against windshield
downtown emerges

誕生

APRIL 15

roads, pipes, power lines
connect us like Indra's net
so taxes pay me

誕生

APRIL 16

post office waiting
line moves imperceptibly -
package flies away

誕生

APRIL 17

Blue blooms peak from ground
covered by snow yesterday.
Days stretch ever long.

誕生

APRIL 18

Spakle where art hung
Brown chairs where black ones just were
Starbucks still sells tea

誕生

APRIL 19

Drive up 94
Once towards home, now away from
There's a toll both ways

誕生

APRIL 20

Tombstones. Just carved rock
that lasts longer than we did.
Hawk glides above me.

誕生

APRIL 21

cracks, bumps, jagged holes
mar the street's smooth start – my bike
rolls along just fine

誕生

APRIL 22

Neighborhood brewpub
Afternoon conversations
Old friends, new faces

誕生

APRIL 23

Bare trees speak of loss.
Nature knows heartbreak. And blue
blossoms fill my yard.

APRIL 24

Cool air, warm sun. Spring
acts like it was always here.
Early moon hangs pale.

誕生

APRIL 25

Crumbled pile of bricks
In a lot where something stood
Walls are just ego

誕生

APRIL 26

Different cafe
Different neighborhood street
Same afternoon lull

誕生

APRIL 27

Another week closed
Siddhartha smiles from his shelf
Oh yeah, there's just now

APRIL 28

garden store starters
getting future tastiness
growing season starts

誕生

APRIL 29

Field Museum collects
the world in one place. Tourists
photograph themselves.

誕生

APRIL 30

Setting sun too bright
to look into. But it makes
the lake so pretty.

誕生

MAY

...I don't think we really notice most changes because they happen gradually and out of our center of focus. Here in the Midwest, we have a saying that if you don't like the weather, all you have to do is wait 5 minutes and it will change. This spring has certainly seen its share of changing weather, with chilly weather hanging around, periodic warm days followed the next by snow (there was a record-setting blizzard in mid-April), and yesterday it was 78 at one point. So yeah, it's gone all over the place.

Some days I worry that I write too many poems about the weather, but I've realized that you could write a poem a day just about the weather here and it would be insightful. The annual cycle of the seasons provides a mirror for so many of the cycles that we experience in our life: birth, death, impermanence, right action, joy, sorrow.

It's a well of inspiration that keeps giving. In fearing that I was writing the same poems I was able to see how the gradual evolution hides the big shifts that do happen: a few months ago I was writing about freezing temperatures and snow, and a few months before that the autumn-inspired contemplation of ending. And now we're in spring and rebirth.

MAY 1

Neighbors say hello.
Warm breeze fills the patio.
Coatlessness feels weird.

MAY 2

Open window brings
spring sounds to my dawn sitting -
Pleasant distractions

MAY 3

clouds darker than night
storm from the West - landing jet
hovers before them

MAY 4

Spring sun warms my face.
My mom lies ill far away.
Practice here! Right now!

MAY 5

Watching the flames leap
at the season's first cook out.
They clean last year's gunk.

MAY 6

Basil, mint, catnip,
thyme - green plants fill my window.
Scents flavor the air.

MAY 7

Pink and white blossoms
burst from branches. And petals
litter below them.

MAY 8

new Wrigleyville seen
through graffiti marked El window
Soul is rarely clean

MAY 9

Dawn sun bounces bright
off a distant building. Gold
ball burns away sleep.

MAY 10

New leaves grasp at wind
They try to catch it. Instead
it blows right through them.

MAY 11

heady perfume fills
the night air - white flowers burst
from sidewalk bushes

MAY 12

Clear skies break through,
moments from where clouds poured rain.
Bunnies munch on grass.

MAY 13

skyline appears as
the highway curves - we come from
and to our mothers

MAY 14

Grey rain fills Monday.
Drops keep falling from new leaves
onto waiting grass.

MAY 15

Names on green street signs
Goethe and Orrington Lunt
No one would know them

MAY 16

one lone tree stands bare
among others flush with green
now is not it's time

MAY 17

sunshine and sadness
are only opposites in
the stories we tell

MAY 18

green leaves will one day
wither and fall - but we don't
take matches to them

MAY 19

Raindrops kiss puddles
Cloud lovers reunited
True royal wedding

MAY 20

I write so many
poems about the weather.
But it's always here.

MAY 21

fog and rain all day
bird hops on my windowsill
eylids droop towards nap

MAY 22

Sink into my bed
El track sparks flash through the night
Bored cat licks her paw

MAY 23

Sit. Be with my mom.
Watch the waves come in and hear
the birds chattering.

MAY 24

pale blue of twilight
hangs soft - street lights flicker on
try to hold back night

MAY 25

Rush hour traffic to
rooftop beer and sausage - grill
man calls our number

MAY 26

Six months to exhale
Rush outside and soak in warmth
We know it won't last

MAY 27

Wake to humid air.
Clothing and skin feels sticky.
Open a window!

MAY 28

hungry cheeping drives
the parents that nest under
the roof of my house

MAY 29

Kids walk home from school
Fill the street with laughing shouts
Days getting longer

MAY 30

late afternoon light,
sudden chorus of rain - then
grey cloudy sunshine?

MAY 31

green green green grass leaves
bushes gardens - I scribble
away at haiku

JUNE

…when I had a chance to finally sit down today, I was reminded of how easy it is to let life get in the way of the things we're looking to do. It made me realize that half (or even more than half) of the victory in this book is that I was able to find some time for writing every day.

It's so easy to let things get in the way of what we want to accomplish. Often, they are very important things. They are things that rightfully clamor for our attention. So the fact that I've written every day, that I've chronicled something every day for over 300 days, is pretty good.

I've gotten better at releasing my attachment to each poem being a masterpiece. In fact, when I work too hard at making a haiku too meaningful, it falls flat. I've found that I have a lot more impact when I let the poem go where it wants to.

Sometimes they are deep, and sometimes they aren't. But that doesn't make any of them better or worse.

May was an emotional month. The haikus were not only describing the timber of my feelings but were helping me process how I wanted to respond. In that, they were as valuable in the writing as I hope they will be in the reading…

JUNE 1

background breeze feels good -
only when it stops do I
notice the silence

JUNE 2

tip of Door County
hike next to same lake as home
but now I can hear

JUNE 3

weekend trip up north
tourists doing tourist stuff
swarmed by mosquitos

日

JUNE 4

My couch feels the same
after a weekend trip. But
I'm three days wiser.

JUNE 5

Neighbor's flower beds
explode in rainbow hues - how
nice of them to share!

JUNE 6

tourists crowd Mag Mile
taking selfies they won't view
locals weave between

JUNE 7

Open house windows.
Feel breeze, hear traffic - direct.
Cat peers out. Watches.

JUNE 8

empty lunch plate - just
savored exotic flavors
all meals end

JUNE 9

storms strewn through the sky
greeted my waking - now sun
fills my afternoon

JUNE 10

the only gringos
in this dive taqueria -
we all speak sabor

JUNE 11

Scattered puddles, soon
to be dry where dry ground was.
Man this beer tastes good!

JUNE 12

train pulled downtown, full
of sleepy eyes and headphones
give our daily bread

JUNE 13

Dogwood tree explodes.
White puffs spiral in the breeze
like snow. I shiver.

日

JUNE 14

computer crashes
commute changes - observing
outside of ownself

JUNE 15

Dawn came long ago
Afternoon streches long arms
Why hibernate now?

JUNE 16

Street fair crowds me - heat,
people, smells, grill smoke - a kid
cries for a sno-cone

JUNE 17

downtown stands hazy
above a jumbled river -
94 creeps slow

JUNE 18

chilled library sits
counterpoint to outside heat
children find escape

JUNE 19

shirt clings to my back
cool fog replaced blazing sun
humidity persists

JUNE 20

dancing at the Drake
marble fountain, sparkling lights
soak in glamour past

JUNE 21

Rain soaks my commute.
Downstate farmers must love it.
Steam rises from tea.

JUNE 22

sun hides behind rain
this year's longest days are grey
mocks my winter dreams

JUNE 23

river flows backwards
through steel and concrete canyon -
sapling under bridge

JUNE 24

El track arteries
connect me to there - but I
don't conduct the train

JUNE 25

ducks sun on their pond
mama leads her ducklings - Bark!
boisterous dog scares them

JUNE 26

a precious moment
these lines try to capture it
birds sing good morning

JUNE 27

small yellow flowers
dot my love's tomato plant -
I whisper to them

JUNE 28

How do I stand now?
Hounded by warlords and fools
Dogen sat zazen.

JUNE 29

Geese sunbathe along
a lakeside pond. Children shout
from the beach just south.

JUNE 30

hazy light streams from
downtown - bats circle for dinner -
I long for a cone

JULY

I'll be straightforward. I've written over 330 haiku. I've written one every day for the last 11 months. It's been on my mind every day. Like, every day. And I'm OK with letting that go.

After all of those poems, I'm realizing that sometimes I'm writing about the same observations because I'm making the same observations. Even for someone who doesn't have the routine of a regular job, life doesn't vary that much. There's a lot of repetition in the experiences that we have, and so yes, I'm going to write about the weather, and the lake, and the train, and the birds.

And the topics that those observations bring to mind haven't varied as much as I thought they would. The range of human emotion isn't as broad as we sometimes think. There's a spectrum, sure, but our lives are not as unique as might imagine.

The end of a journey is a natural point of reflection. And while July is rarely thought of as the ending of anything, this year it is for me. That gets to the heart of the project for me. It's just one more way it gave me a reason to pay attention to what was happening around me.

My job then is to observe July like I would look out the windows of taxi taking me to the airport after a vacation in a foreign country. Soak it in. Try to squirrel it away in my mind while knowing that I still won't remember much. And try to scribble a few notes about my favorite things…

JULY 1

sweat drips down my back
warm breeze flutters leaves - sled waits
still in the corner

JULY 2

green light go red light
stop - thousands of small hearts beat
unseen til one breaks

JULY 3

Heat ripples over
tracks that stretch past and future.
Bell snaps me present.

JULY 4

fireworks pop as dusk falls
crowds stream to catch the big show
I'm free to not mind

JULY 5

rain smells float heavy
grey cloud collage drifts above
we wander post-4th

JULY 6

Cars pass train station
My bike leans on bus stop sign
Sun beams feel so good

JULY 7

weekend morning cut -
early lawnmower - I sit
annoyed and impressed

JULY 8

Newly lit coals smoke.
Pause. Listen. The infinite
lies before dinner.

JULY 9

evening sun reflects
off downtown skyline - shadows
lengthen into night

JULY 10

Bodies sway in sync.
Ride to work. Can the day be
extraordinary?

JULY 11

man mortars new house
avenues stretch through heat
beers shared after work

JULY 12

Lake front ride offers
same lake as last year. But it's
not the same water.

JULY 13

Flash of orange on green
King pauses his fluttering
Makes a leaf his throne

JULY 14

Dairy Star Snow Blitz
A moment in a hot day
How tasty it is!

JULY 15

wind whips trees, sky turns
storm unloads rain in a burst -
humidity sticks

JULY 16

wind whips trees, sky turns
storm unloads rain in a burst -
humidity sticks

JULY 17

My sunburn peels off
leaving new, pink skin. Headlines
shout latest outrage.

JULY 18

Train rocks me homeward
Orange blue clouds mark westward sky
Next is not here yet

JULY 19

life-saving box beeps
gives time and takes time from her
she teases the nurse

JULY 20

Curtains billow in,
bluster - replaced by steady
drops on my window

JULY 21

weeds blossom color
where they were pulled last summer
waiting sun peaks out

JULY 22

street corner gardens
stray bright bursts as we pass by
sunflowers stand tall

JULY 23

deepest purple dusk
moment passes past violet
alley light calls moths

JULY 24

Sun over O'Hare
Storms elsewhere, delay stretches.
So many accents.

JULY 25

Manhattan twilight
people, sidewalks, buildings, rain
It feels different

JULY 26

sidewalks and subways
defined by the souls who pass
through them between points

JULY 27

Clouds drift through blue skies
Bits of sky peek through white clouds
Waves lap at the shore

JULY 28

sunrise brushes grave
markers soft pink - the dead don't
know their own beauty

JULY 29

neighborhood street fair
trampled beer cups replace cars
brief pause til Monday

JULY 30

same sun warms my face
ducklings paddle in circles
car radio blares

JULY 31

ghost moon in blue sky
sits quietly so look up
your poem waits ready

GOODBYE, SAFE TRAVELS

At the end of any trip, there's the moment of goodbye. It's the liminal point where you go from being a traveler to, well, whatever comes next. So now it's time for us to go on to the next stage.

We really don't stop being travelers, though, do we? We go from journey to journey, sometimes not even realizing that one has stopped, and another started. Or we look back at all our travels and realize that they were really just legs of one long trip.

Thank you for joining me on my voyage through the year in this great city, this unruly conglomeration of people, animals, trains, buildings, weather, and relationships. I'm not sure what the next journey will bring for me, but I'm so glad you joined me on this one. And wherever you are going, I wish you insightful days and peaceful nights.

AND THANK YOU

Over the course of a year, my wife put up with me regularly staring off into the distance while counting syllables on my fingers. For that, and for not looking at me funny when I announced I was going to write a book of haiku, I'm thankful. She is the perfect demanding flower.

I posted many of these poems on social media throughout the year. Thank you to everyone who read them and gave a quick like or comment (especially Dave who gave a thumbs up to just about every poem). It did much to bolster my confidence and made it feel a little less lonely.

Years ago, I spent some time going to the Green Mill Lounge on Sunday nights for the weekly Poetry Slam. It reignited a love that I had for language that had lain dormant for a long time. It's been a while since I've been back but I'm grateful to Marc Smith and the community for showing me that poetry can still be vibrant and relevant.

Thank you to Michiyo and Joe Fingerhut for making sure none of my kanji said "Chicken Soup"

My partners at JETLAUNCH.net have continued to help me create self-published works that look amazing. It's nice knowing you have a team you can rely on.

My friends and family continue to be wonderful companions on this journey through the world. I'm looking forward to many more trips around the sun with all of them.

ABOUT DAVID

David J.P. Fisher isn't a professional poet, but he'd like to play one on TV. He's written 7 books of the non-fiction business persuasion, but this is his first published volume of poetry. You can reach him at dfish@davidjpfisher.com or through Twitter @dfishrockstar.